The Stone Cicada

and Other Poems

My thanks to The University of Michigan Biology Department for permission to use the illustration on which the image of the cicada on the cover of this book is based.

The Stone Cicada

and Other Poems

by Leonard Wolf

— Medusa Press —

Copyright

First published in 2001 by The Medusa Press, PMB 396,
61 East 8th Street, New York, NY 10003

Copyright © 2001 by Leonard Wolf

Library of Congress Cataloging-in Publication Data

Wolf Leonard.
The Stone Cicada: a collection of poems by Leonard Wolf
    1. Poems I. Title

ISBN 0-9707074-0-1

Book Design by Lauren Horwitz
Printed in Hong Kong by Best Set Typesetter, Ltd.

Note

Many of the poems included here have previously appeared in the following magazines:

Accent Magazine, The Antioch Review, The Atlantic Monthly, Commentary, Contact Magazine, The Colorado Quarterly Review, Commonweal, Furioso, Harper's Magazine, The Hudson Review, The Literary Review Mademoiselle, The New Mexico Quarterly Review, The New Yorker, The Northwest Review, Poetry: Chicago, The Sewanee Review, The Virginia Quarterly Review, The Yale Review.

Books by Leonard Wolf

Poetry:
Hamadryad Hunted

Fiction:
The False Messiah
The Glass Mountain

Non-Fiction:
Voices from the Love Generation
The Passion of Israel
A Dream of Dracula
Bluebeard: The Life and Crimes of Gilles de Rais
Horror: A Connoisseur's Guide to Literature and Film
Dracula: The Connoisseur's Guide

Books Edited:
The Uses of the Present
The Annotated Dracula
The Annotated Frankenstein
Wolf,s Complete Book of Terror
Sheridan Le Fanu: Selected Tales
Doubles, Dummies, and Dolls
The Essential Jekyll and Hyde
The Essential Phantom of the Opera
Blood Thirst

Translated from the Yiddish:
Itzik Manger's *The Book of Paradise*
Itzik Manger: *Selected Poetry and Prose*
Der Nister's *The Family Mashbir*
Israel Rabon's *The Street*
Isaac Bashevis Singer's *The Certificate*
Yiddish Folktales
Poems included in *The Penguin Book of Yiddish Verse* and
A Treasury of Yiddish Poetry

Translated from the French:
Gaston Leroux's *The Phantom of the Opera*
Theophile Gautier's *Amorous Death*

Translated into Yiddish:
Winnie the Pooh (*Vini der Pu*)

Two Words To the Reader:

The poems in this collection appear in alphabetical order. My only excuse for such an arrangement is that I would like each poem to be read as an event in itself, independent of chronology.

There are occasional references in the poems to Carley Ridge, a sparsely settled area in the foothills of northern California where I lived for a while; and to Persia, where I lived for a year.

This book is dedicated to my grandchildren,
Yardena, Rosa, Eitan and Joseph who, I hope,
will read it when they are grown up.

How To Begin

From a recipe by Ari the Learned in his twelfth-century *Book of the Icelanders*

To make a poem, catch a goat;
Draw a knife across its throat.

When all life has left the creature,
Skin it; dip its hide in water.

Add old lime and stir the pot
Till the mixture seems to clot.

Then throw the clotted stuff away
And add fresh water every day

For a week, in winter more.
When the water's clean and clear,

Make a frame to stretch the skin,
Set well away from heat and sun.

Let it dry, then moisten it
And scrape the skin when it is wet.

On the flesh side of the skin
Pour fine pumice, rub it in.

Now make the skin tight in the frame
And wait a day before you trim

The vellum you have made. Then scan
The sky for raven, goose, or swan

(Some bird of size that does not sing)
And pluck a feather from a wing.

A left-wing feather if you can
Because such feathers fit the hand.

For ink, you need the bearberry,
And bark stripped from a willow tree.

Boil the mixture. When you spill
A drop that forms a little ball,

The ink is done. The vellum waits
The issue of the murdered goat,

The plundered raven, swan, and tree,
The music of the bearberry.

Table of Contents

Adam

This is how it really happened: she ate; he ate,
Then they tumbled down into a swoon.
While they slept, the angels came and set
Everything different in the stately room.

Waking, he noticed that the furniture
Had been taken away. The Louis XVIth bed,
The escritoire and Irish linen were
Gone, but the Salvation Army had

Sent other things. Weakly, the morning came
Like failing light. He tried to pray
But would not, when she stirred against him
In a curious and awkward way

That roused him to her woeful loveliness:
Part child, part woman and part nakedness.

*

Adultery

Sits by the fireplace, the seducer talks
Of trouble in the heart, until he weeps
Before the woman, virtuous, whose hand,
Soft and gentle, delicate and long
Marks a moment of compassion when
His kiss falls on her and disaster strikes
Them backward to an unmade distant bed
Where consolation and confusion roll
Sweetly, swiftly toward disaster. Passion
Roars, and self-denial is a squeaking
Beast that nips the lovers in the heel
As lips, devotion, breasts, and sightless eyes
With lassitude in one convulsion join
To pity, wonderfully, the peevish groin.

*

Air Mail

The summer is stingy, long and hot this year.
Even the nettles are finding it hard
Scrabbling in an August with no rain.

And California has turned dry. Far
Away to the east, weeds in another yard
Flourish. Growing is a pain

In both directions. Father lives
In Cleveland, where I grew
Swiftly, thin, morose and tall.

Summers were hot and wet. He grieves
Because I've wandered west and do
Not write. He loves to talk, and tells me all

The news. There's thunder every day; the lake
Is more polluted now than when I swam
In the pollution I recall. He says

My mother means to cut her hair to make
Her headaches stop. My nervous brother came
Home from the hospital too soon. The daze

He walks in may turn violent. He seems
Waiting for a moment to explode
Against my father and the steady heat.

My sister gathers green stamps and redeems
Them twice a year for imitation Spode
Or copper-bottomed pots. She won't eat meat

And uses canvas shoes with rubber soles.
My father says that sex is on her mind.
He also says that I deserve more troubles

Than I've got, but he consoles
Me with the truth that time and sorrows find
Their victim out, however he rebels.

He thinks I should come home and take my place
In Cleveland with my kin. I write to say
The varnished truth— that I am well and glad

To hear from him, as always; that I miss
The family, but cannot get away
This year to visit, though I wish I could.

I sign the letter "Love" and mail it. Late
At night, in bed, I think how letters fly
Easily into the dark— on wings.

*

The Allegory of the Cave

The necromancer in his cave decides
To quench illusion, since he means to die
At last an honest man, therefore he guides
An ivory stick against his keen left eye.

Bleeding is a way to tell the truth
And drown illusion, so he puts his hand
Against the second eyeball in its sheath
Of bone, and pokes it with his ivory wand.

Now he is blind, the cave is cool, serene.
There is no further animal to wound.
A moment follows of pure calm, and then
His brain hurts like a rainbow underground.

But oh, the inoffensive jelly's gone
That caught so deftly for the sense bright light;
The empty caverns round the ragged bone
Ache with emptiness instead of sight.

The necromancer's shadowed to his grave
By specters waggling from his poor scarred mind.
He meddled far too long in Plato's cave
And drank the shadows Plato left behind.

*

The Angels to Lot

Deny the city when it rears and shows
The loins of Sodom. Deny the prose
The city-dwellers in their temples speak:
Howling Hebrew or inchoate Greek.

Leave! The high-reared walls of clay
Will stumble backward, and the towers decay;
The fountains steam, the royal palace scorch
Beneath the action of God's cleansing torch.

The town will yell. The stripling king will send
A pleading virgin or a young prebend
To ask your prayers, but you know the place
Is dead already and this foul-mouthed race

Is done. Be shrewd; be swift. To Zoar, go
With ass and oxen. You've no time to show
Your daughters to the city. And why make
The least small gesture for the city's sake?

Be swift and go. Your daughters do not need
Involved instruction. Later, they will breed
Up generations. And the coming fault
Will not be incest at the last, but salt.

✳

6

Archimago

It was a sweet French voice cried out in the sun,
"Children, children, come away from the door,
Children, children, come away, come away."

High in the alley, where that cry
Pushed on its way, another voice sang
On the roof clearly, over the tile.

The sun, polishing jasmine, and the door
Kept the children in the glow
Of their brief ignorance of song.

Behind the door, and on that roof,
Forbidden singer, not their mother, high
Before their wonder, set her proud

Resistant singing in a key
Fit to become an avatar
And whirl the children through the door.

The mother, from the hollow evil called,
"Children, children, come away,
Children, children, come away from that door."

From the mote and brilliance of the place
Where evil in its brightness cooled the beam
Of their delight, the children came,

Came to the mother in her shadowed lights
Who loved against the stranger where she sang
And closed the arch and image of their door.

*

Baudelaire (I)

"Joy," he said, "is the most vulgar
Of ornaments." He thought his brain
Was a mirror, bewitched. He prayed
And prayed, and prayed
To a black panther, yellow-eyed and lame.

The exquisite beauty of a hurt
Animal turned loose upon the streets
Of Paris chastened him. Spleen,
Spleen turned holy in the art
Of love, and Satan foolish in

The art of poetry. He heard
A growling! Like a carpenter,
Against disruption of the soul he used
Wounds, anthrax, sutures, gangrene
And hot-house tulips. A miracle

Of concentration for a man in trouble
To build a tower of joy
Upon the vulgar coast of pain.
Makeshift! makeshift! and the sea,
Quotidian as hell, lapped round

The fort where he was safe—
Or would have been, except he breached
Himself the postern gate. Black, black,
The panther limped along the coast
And nightly entered in.

*

9

Baudelaire (II)

Suppose him living in marshes with a sick
Headache named Gille de Raies inside
His head: the good looking murderer for trouble;
Undulant bracken for his bed.

Then, disease. Slow disease in Paris,
Like a decaying butterfly. Rimbaud
Went to the jungle, took his pocket torch
And strolled into the darkness. Baudelaire

Stayed home. He had the pavement, hot
As cobblestones to spit on; and sick friends.
He had, also, his angel, not yet
Invested with his soul, struggling

Like a bubble in a marsh to rise,
To burst into an exhalation, sweet,
Sweet as the flesh the dying poet
Wore, and most melodious.

Something of victory the angel won
When it abandoned its precise milieu
For music. As for defeat,
The intricate voyager among the damned

Found no place quite like home and worked,
Half mirror and half man, to be
Sick as a dog in the devoted dark,
Sound as a bell on the Parisian quai.

✳

Birthdays

So then, I threaten and bluster,
I say to each year, "I am here.
Take note of me, I am master
Of this and of that and of fear."

But a clock ticks on in a tower,
Bragadoccio declines into blame,
A hand breaks the back of my hour,
And a child keeps misspelling my name

And the fear, of which I was master
Lolls in my house half asleep
And yawns when I threaten and bluster
Lazy, but ready to leap;

And the voice that I lashed into bluster
Goes "baa" like a dutiful sheep.

*

California Autumn

Nothing in California but November
To bring us around. The thin air, graying,
Informs of change. Elsewhere, I remember
Season's breaking sharp— or ice, playing
No mock eternity, as here. Then brown
Hits us in September. Later white snapped
Fangtooth and breathless. All around
The gullies moved November, wrapped us

Close with change and white. All until March
There was no argument. The green and white
In gusts tussled the month away. Both harsh,
The unicorn and lion raged, affright
With wild, unstrictured time. That month long rage
Was fierce for us and hard, but time moved on
Like an unwelcome lesson, page by page,
Which, learned, the chapter closed, was done.

Now, nothing in California but November,
Month name, slipping disgrace across the calendar,
Brings us around, but slyly, to remember
Time. Here, the month so unparticular
And changeless, makes time a rigid Pegasus,
An unwinged public horse we sit astride,
A mock-eternal beast that carries us
Round California carousels we ride.

✳

Charlotte

Hartshorn! the spirits in a lady's chamber
Aged. The tousled garments of her speaking
Season, purple in color. Gilt-embossed
The chest of her mementoes: beads of amber,
Simulacra of her voyage, carved; and Peking
Fans, soft Delhi bells; except the one thing lost
Somewhere in the shuffle, in the mangled rubrics
Hanging from the walls. Soapstone and jade--
The intelligent objects and the frail now mix
In her proportions. Fine and vague, afraid,
She guards herself at night against attack
And pillows, like a weapon, her *seicento* pistol;
Her hands are beautiful; despite its crack,
Her mind is sometimes like a Swedish crystal.

*

Chicken Little

After the blow of liberation
Came the chick,
Happy in his happy hour,
Free to watch the tile fall from the roof
And draw his moral.

A little yellow chick,
No bigger than an egg,
With plenty to think about,
A very good head on his shoulders,
Ready to spread the news.

He was swindled by prefiguration.

By a trick of sky
Making a show of power;
He grew to chicken, torpid and aloof,
A bird of quarrel.

Now, he, bigger than a chicken coop,
A very firm head on his shoulders,
Tiresias in the hen-yard, wrong
About Apocalypse,
Snarls at the least occasion
And vilifies the news.

*

Christmas Eve

Sometimes the king, sometimes the queen, of heaven
Looks down; sometimes the skeptic, hesitant,
Looks upward with a rooster's quarrelsome
Eye. But most, when the December
Days begin to huddle in the pen
Of the declining year he casts his eye
Upward, warily, to find the sun—
The skeptic, lost in Heliopolis
In winter peering for a sign from heaven—

And does not get it! Until Christmas eve,
His soul gone crotchety with disbelief,
He stands unsteady in the throbbing snow
To watch a musical believer run
Full-throated and abandoned toward the arms
Of love. The tunnel in the falling
Snow grows luminous where passed the carol
And the caroler announcing God
In the highest, and on earth His peace.

All may be well! The skeptic and the sun,
Together with the singer lost in snow
In Heliopolis at Christmas time
Are patient syllables of an unspoken
Word. The snow is caught; it twists
One final moment in a fit of light
Before it settles; and the time of year
Is Christmas, and the time of day
A white approximation of a world.

✳

Classics

Students know the name of Oedipus,
Know his disaster, where it grinds
The lanterns, sparkling, of his Grecian flesh.

The classroom shines; each mother's son
Made helpless by the dazzle, shades his eyes—
He has an inkling he has seen Jocasta perish.

The mother's daughters of another mind
And mood are harder eyed, receive the shock
Of distant gods and their perverse exactions,

Guard their brothers from the eidolon,
The size implacable of tense priapus.
None evolves a word, turn Christian faces

Twisted for an instant in a strange king's rages
To an embattled calm. The classroom waits
The passage of an hour and twenty pages

When their instructor to a saner climate shifts
And to a better god. Once free of Greeks
Light warms them from a burning bush they find

Inside a darker text whose landscape shows
The fulgurations and the brimstone traces
Of luminous, abominable Hebrew places.

*

The Continent

In Africa, in Africa,
The continent holds still
Beneath its madmen and the sea,
Beneath the bloody owl.

The leopard, out of doors,
Leaps yelling, through the wrack,
Runs with the jungle like a leash
Of vine around his neck.

Salt water wears away
All Africa in stages;
Inland, twelve saints defray
Their board and wages.

Those twelve, in huts, come in
To bind up wounds.
The leopard howls, begins
Impure but perfect sounds.

Inside, twelve beggars move;
Unclean, with trembling hands
They walk in restless rooms
And bind up wounds,

While tambour of the sea
Beats harsh, and timeless, stale
Behind the melody
Of jackals where they wail.

Good! How good, and who?
In the contrivances of grass,
Frail unbelievers in a church
The twelve prepare a mass

And bow. Out in the dark,
The leopard in the swale
And the hyena bark
While Africa turns pale

Or black— whichever shade
That continent demands
Whose sick are holy made
By their imperfect hands.

*

The Cookie Witch

Jasmine-scented May still troubles me
With danger of that night I seemed to run
Through darkness in a wood while Gretel held,
Too reasonable sister, cool, my hand.

It happened in a dream or in a song:
Deep in an oaken forest we pursued
A golden cookie witch until she turned
To love us gently in the darkened wood.

Cookie jar and raisins in the gloom,
She had been childless for an ancient age;
I loved her without doubt, and she became
My sweet-toothed cookie mother in the shade.

O spiteful sister! She would not believe
The golden cookie witch was good and fair,
Would care for us in forests, like the birds,
Would warm us in the dark and feed us there.

My sister Gretel lied. There is no gloom
So dark as that in which we murdered her
Who would have warmed us in our utmost need,
And fed us sweetmeats that we hungered for.

In May, death-dealing Gretel tore the flesh
Of the best creature in the wilderness.
Her blood was sweet as any dream or song,
And jasmine tells me of my sister's wrong.

*

The Corn Crake

The corn crake in the sun! I heard her cry
Too near my book. Willingly, I sent
My prayers out, my lament.
Unwillingly, I watched her die.

Only an ugly bird in harvest, with a wing
Forlorn and broken, like a stick—
"A kind of land rail," unto dying sick,
Nor breath in that brown throat, to sing.

How shall a bird be praised? It needs
A hush of sunlight and three wheeling larks.
Here, a gleaner in the stubble marks
A tattered circle in the barley seeds.

The corn crake in a shaft of light expires
As larks insult her, singing to conceal
Such praise as I can give. They turn, they wheel
Like demons plunging into separate fires.

Melodious larks, into the sunlight grand
Fly exulting toward the painted west.
The land rail stiffens in a kind of nest
Of feathers waving in the scattered sand.

*

Country Crofts

Every croft makes me remember
My childhood's chamber
Where all that I loved best
Between three books was pressed.

There was a thorn and thistle,
And an oaten whistle;
The goosegirl's ugly mother,
And her youngest brother.

There, each trick and stranger
Filled my room with danger;
With Merlin and his trouble,
And kettle's cauldron bubble.

It was a joy to see
Such village husbandry:
My swineherds and my churchyard and my hen,
My sturdy and my Robin-hooded men.

Thorn for me and nettle,
And Lancelot's cold mettle
Made my crofts to be
Full of minstrelsy.

Sweet ambergris and amber
Filled my childhood's chamber
With bay leaves and with sorrel,
With asphodel and laurel.

Now croft makes me remember
That golden chamber,
But I can pay no fee
Restores that minstrelsy.

I can search in nettle,
In every hut and wattle,
But cannot find my hen,
My Merlin, or my gallant-hooded men.

*

The Courtship

The wasted housewife who must overreach
To justify her day. How fair she was!
Beneath his gaze, she fluttered on a beach
Of golden sand and was a golden girl
With breasts emboldened to the darkling sea;
Until he broke her, as a merman does,
Upon his loins. She watched the breakers swirl
Salt and bloodshed for a golden girl
And ran the length of an encircling bay
Until he got and pierced her to the ground
With cries like seagulls leaping from his lips
And drowned her, drowned her in the crimson sand
Where overreaching, on that shore, like blood
Creeping sweetly down her thighs began.

*

Coyote: On Carley Ridge

Last night, coyote streaked across the ridge.
I almost did not see them, but their howl
Of desolation echoed in the dry
Creek bed. They gave their misery an edge
Of contemplation, as if foul
Intentions against flesh had shaped their cry

First with intelligence, and then remorse
To form a penitent, unholy sound
Against the sky. Later, I heard
Them cough judiciously around my horse,
Like old men talking horseflesh, who have found
A stud worth praising with a word

Or two. I fell asleep, but woke
Again to hear coyote in the pack
Howling in full pursuit. Once more their cry
Rose from the ragged throat of misery
And begged for pity while they shed the blood
Of some caught creature in the neighborhood.

Then silence. In the morning, they were gone
And I had leisure to observe what food
Their damned eternal pity fed upon.

*

Crows— Shiraz

Crows in the lemon trees say, "gnaw, gnaw."
Hurting their throats it seems to me with "gnaw,"
So violent, so raucous in the morning.

The sun is working in the trees, whose fruit,
Early in the spring is small and green.
The crows encourage growth, they cry out, "gnaw."

I hear them every morning when I come
Into the garden where I hide and wait.
They see me coming and cry, "gnaw."

That's fellow feeling! By the dozens, they
Utter round me their delighted praise
Of me, themselves, the garden. They sing, "gnaw."

They've loved me now six mornings in a row
Because I come so early where they are.
They love me for my ears. They cry out "gnaw."

Politely, if I could, I would say, "Crows,
Thank you for your song, your joy, your love,
Your wild excitement and your clacking pride."

In English, I would add what else is true—
"I haunt this early garden, you damned crows,
Because I know there is a nightingale

That cowers somewhere in the lemon trees
Waiting for silence between 'gnaw' and 'gnaw'
To spill an instant of its grieving song."

*

The Dervish and the Horse

My horse moves under the sun with a wise patience
Learned of his ancestors who also climbed
Among these burning hills. We ride past grape-vines
Stuck in the soil, like twisted wires
Whose shadows, morning and evening, writhe and knot
Close to the bony root. The land is dry;
The favorite bird that flies appears to be
The crow, though vultures circle overhead.

The dervish whom I visit in his cave
Says I will look like Persia soon. My beard
Is straggling and my eyes are growing dull
Like his and I no longer blink against
The sun. The bitter taste of limestone dust
And nervous smells of villages do not
Offend me as they did when first I came
Riding, a sort of pilgrim, to these hills.

He says the land will teach me. In patches where
The earth becomes ashamed of dryness, water
Breaks unwillingly from rocks, or else
Is drawn by leading strings from mountains down
To heat-worn villages and fields. Soon,
Nightingales will come to join the crows;
Together, they will show me images
I would not dare when there were only crows.

My horse and I beat at the earth. The dervish
Sleeps in it. My horse is merely innocent.
He is prepared to stand or walk or die.
The dervish says to listen, but I think
This soil, with its bad habit of survival
And despair is not equipped for truth;
Though I can well believe there is a voice
Like whispering cicadas that can tell

Of lingering evasions, half-hearted hopes,
Sunlight, barley, vultures, hawks and crows;
The painful, pitiful attempts of goats
To stand like stallions carved against the sky.
This is a land where bowstrings have not twanged
With any sense for fifteen hundred years.
The dervish hears his cracked voice pray for me;
I pray for him and ride away, estranged.

*

Diana

Toward midnight, bearing in her hand
A pomegranate,
Beautiful Diana suddenly appeared.

Do not misunderstand,
She said,
It is the pomegranate

I have brought.

With her other hand
The girl undid
The clasp of her so fragrant gown.

At midnight, long past midnight,
I could eat
The waspish kernels of that ruby fruit.

By then, Diana in the snowy bed
Had spilled, so late, so warm
The smallest sprinkle of her tears.

*

The Egg

There are days, like today,
This minute,
When I fall in love
With an egg.
Its seamlessness,

The easy way in which
It stands for
Almost anything.
Life.
Protective wobbling.
Breakfast.

For logicians,
The egg's
Simplicity
Insults the mind.
An egg,

By no means
Circular,
Imitates the circle
Having no
Beginning and no end.

Ask that conundrum,
God, the first
Egg maker
Who worked
Without tools

Achieving a fine
Mat finish and any number
Of colors
From which come
Cluckers and flyers that sing.

Ask Him how,
Facing that smoothness
So unlike a face
And yet implying
Faces

Every way it turns—
How was
The beautiful
The beautiful
Egg made?

*

The Ethics of My Fathers

Rabbi Hillel, blessed be his name,
Pitying the world has said,
"In a place where there are no men,
Try to be a man."

It was also he who observed
(With great effect on me who am
Inclined to corpulence):
"The more flesh, the more worms."

Living in a country of few men and much
Flesh, it has been hard to tell
Just where my duties lay
If I would honor Hillel.

But, God be praised, rabbis we have enough!
Reb Akiba, that undying fountain
Of pure pity writes in the same book
That wisdom prospers in the silent man.

*

The Exiles

We reached the ancient desert,
There sat down;
The group of us sat down.

We were a band of exiles
Left behind
Or pilgrims gone ahead
To reach a happier time.

For us the gourd tree did not grow,
There was no raven in the sun,
Nor any crow.

We prayed
As if the tiger in our midst
With yellow eye
Was a tiger sent from God,
And we could pray.

The tiger stretched his stripes
Out in the sun,
The jackals fawned on him,
He did not make them run.

There was one in the heat
Cried out that we could beat
A stone to make the water run,
And so outwit the sun.

The tiger showed no haste;
There was no stone or stick
In all that waste;
Nothing at all to beat
Except the tiger in the heat.

That night the stars came out,
And Arab dead, in hosts
Came to claim our ghosts,
Wrapped round in burnooses,
Wrapped round in burnooses,
As if in shrouds.

*

Fan Mail

I have a friend who writes,
"These days, your poems
Stink of death." That's
Friendship for you— a loving

Truce, broken by raids
Of candor. No doubt
My friend is right, but it's
Not kind to send her mean-

Eyed horse into my garden
Where he pounds with iron
Hoofs my peonies,
My roses and my ferns

Into a wad of death.
I say it isn't fair.
She knows, she knows I did
Not write my garden.

*

Ficino

Acoutered like the race of pandars' prince,
Ficino takes the valley in his stride;
He is the dwarf to conquer elephants,
A crooked blaster of rhinocerous hide.

It is the hunting season, and he takes
A double barreled shotgun and a dog
That wears a silver bell around its neck,
And hobbles after, like a palsied frog.

The hound dog's bauble in the valley sounds
To fig trees, to wild rosemary, to thyme,
But will not echo, as if spiders bound
To silence death's resounding on the vines.

The valley hovers like a sacrifice
That waits for a priest's orisons to end;
Ficino's out to treble, in his eyes,
A stature some few inches out of mend.

And lo! Nine swallows in the dwarf's clear sky,
Two barrels in the shotgun at his back;
One mongrel, crippled, at the hunter's side
That wears a silver toy around its neck.

Nine swallows, troubled, in Ficino's sky,
Then eight resisting birds hooked to the air;
Then five! With what ventriloquies
He tricks the barrels to his shrewd affair.

Then none. The hound dog's trinket rings,
It breaks and jangles like a crazy bell.
And echoes, tearing from the spiders' webs
Slash the valley where the swallows fell.

*

A Field Guide to the Western Birds

Long ago, I read the other poets, and
To tell the truth, I envied them
For having a country, talking of the land
According to its dirt and cornstalks, names
Of wild flowers, counties, fenceposts, stones or mules
And charming accents of the village fools.

It seemed too bad for me whose memories
Of childhood were a speechless town
And no arroyos. The disabilities
Of English second-hand, an idiom
Half-Shelley and half-Yiddish throttled me
Before I risked a line of poetry.

But risked it just the same— a flair
Of ignorance was still a flair. I wrote
As best I could, avoiding Nature
And the rural life, though I could quote—
And did— *A Field Guide to the Western Birds*
When my first skylark sang to my first words.

"O! noble-bosomed Hawk!" I had my hero
Cry in an important place— and I
Was reared in Cleveland where the smokestacks throw
A universal nationality
Of soot across the landscape, and my speech
The standard English that the high schools teach.

Language is hard, and I confess I still
Envy the straw tucked in the poet's mouth
Though I have heard Rebekah at the well
At Nahor when the servant from the south
Breathed the excellence of Isaac's name
And she turned beautiful and bright with shame.

*

Flight: On Carley Ridge

My hand held it. Its fine teeth
Trembling in a venom of decay
Chittered through the syllables of death.

Too bad, too late. I caught that wandering
Bat, as if my hand caught pain
Bewildered into fur, and fluttering.

Staring out of envy into hate,
Its mouse's eyes, like speckles of bright flint,
Steadily corroded toward defeat.

I let it go. There was a moment, soiled
And nervous as it twitched its shroud
Of wings and would not fly. Hurt, spoiled,

It fumbled into air, where twice it cried
Then swooped, insanely silent, till it died.

*

Florentine Easter (I)

I

The city of Florence in the marble seen
Palazzos shows; and sunlight, ponderous
As massive gold, shines heavily between
Red balustrades. In alleys, perilous
With beauty, Cleveland glows, a nebulous
And distant structure in Italian air;
A reasonable town, not dangerous
At Easter time. Its traveler, shy, takes care
Of Florence with its God and His imposing snare.

II

The city of Florence is a broken stone
That shines in fragments on the Arno plain.
A ruined crypt that may be looked upon
By any tourist at the risk of pain.
The godless Clevelander, in towers, vain
With the besotted vanity of years
Explores the wreck of the intense inane.
The city printed on a card, brings tears;
Its print in stone brings love and grave religious fears.

III

He wants no god. In Florence where he turns
Are mumbling priests, and on the butcher's hooks
Hang lambs adorned with roses. Florence burns
The thickest incense; prints the fairest books
Of prayers for her cathedrals. There, Christ looks
Compassion crudely from a monument
And cherubs, grimy in their dusty nooks
Adore him, simpering, from a pediment
Where all the knees of Florence in His praise are bent.

IV

Who eats this eats wrath, or perfect life,
Or else the crumbs that fall from it betray
The baker's weakness, or the baker's wife
Who makes thin wafers that too soon decay.
The Clevelander is glad the rich array
Before the altar's tarnished, and a rent
Is in the altar cloth. He tastes the clay
That's in the bread and knows no God is pent
In musty wafers waiting with malign intent.

V

The queen of Sheba is another queen!
But Christ in Florence in an emperor, wan,
Denied her presence. Busy Florentines
Have time to watch her, and her purple swan
Making their progress. Who has looked upon
That black lady with her leopard's eyes
May not be saved. Unless his soul outrun,
With heaven's help, her Abyssinian sighs,
He'll trip in luxury and lose his paradise.

VI

Imagination's paradox. To sin
Where we adore, and by remote decree
To maim the god we have salvation in.
The north is brutal; from the nearest tree
The Norsemen hang him; in the south, we see
Him clinging gently. From his side, a dew
Like ichor flowing, while humility
In every picture more intense than true
Sustains him where he hangs, his palms pierced through
        and through.

VII

He'll have no gods; the Cleveland tourist, now
A wide-eyed truant from a safer shore
Is still erect. No image sees him bow,
Except his head, rebelliously, before
The beautiful. His lips will not implore
A resurrection. Swiftly, swiftly flows
The stream of his impiety. The more
The church in satin and in triumph goes,
The deeper roils his current and more fierce it grows.

VIII

The traveler lives in Cleveland O. How shall
He bear such knowledge gracefully; he stands
Amazed before these icons that appall
His reason. Yet his intellect commands
Lake Erie's troubled and ungracious strands
Without much shock. There, limestone slakes the ore
Unhelped by attitudes of praying hands.
In Florence, it makes fountains from which pour
Out streams of grace and glory at the church's door.

IX

Die down! The church is a presumption torn
Out of the mouths of babes. Belief must die,
And prayer too. He's bought a missal, worn
By an Italian hand, whose pages lie
In soft black letter to his heart and eye
And lovely, with the classic innocence
Of lies that are believed. Abashed, he'll buy
Tomorrow, on the grain of a pretence
A gaudy rosary and count him out of sense.

X

Why will the stones rise up and Duomo build
Whose source is beauty, peril and decay?
Poor Clevelander; he's busy, and has filled
His notebooks sternly for a later day
When his emotions, after long delay
And recollected, like a dream appear
Which there impelled him, while he could, to pray
Away from Cleveland. In a single year
He will deny that too; and he denies it here.

✴

Florentine Easter (II)

Gets hence on Sunday for his poem's sake,
Poet to the streets like a schismatic;
Wraps bell, book and candle in a hide
Of Paschal lamb inside an attic.

Precise, the bells go off; the poem wavers
In the interstices of air that bells obscure.

The old world, like an orphan, fetches him
With towers, pauper-prince and beggar's cry
To pay whatever alms require the poem,
Whatever metaphors the stones imply.

(In Amsterdam, the Sunday merchants crown
The labors of their week with guilders;
In London, in Cat's Alley, cinema
Keeps Cinderella from her pile of cinders.)

The Sunday air goes off, the poem's sake
Still wavers in the hang-bells like a poppet.

The poem is let go, and Sunday time
Tolls like dragging bells beneath the ocean;
Sunlight turning black-eyed Susans blind
Sears both continents with imprecision.

(Shines on, the same world's sun. And nothing stirs.
The poet is the butt of his contagion
Who feels his poem move, like dying bees
Before a sweet occasion.)

Bell, book and candle in the lambskin lie,
Unplacid suns to Easter cities come;
The poet of the dread elections tries
In Florence how to keep his poems dumb.

*

Florentine Sonnet

Whose creed is this, where, narrowly, the bells
Implore for peace inside a city? Shades
And palaces confused with darkness, spill
Among the stones and penitents. The dead,

The dead come up like dusty pallbearers
To ape the living; labor in their sleep
To be alive, but hurried from their graves
They hunt salvation, like their baptisms, cheap.

Intent to pray, and in battalions, swift
They swoop on Florence. Let the city, hard,
Cling to its turrets, and the priests maintain
More perfect vigils, and their chapels guard

Against the dead who pray. O, terrible
Their voices when awake; how, in a dream
Shall they be gentle, who, incredible,
Speak like the swaying artifacts they seem.

The sleepers rage and cross themselves alive.
They murmur "*deus*" like a curse profound
Or "*pace, pace*", until wild, they shake
The shutters desperate for a living sound.

Confusion whispers in the cobblestones
At Easter time. The living speak no ill
Of the defiling dead. The creed absolves
The moving only, while the dead hold still.

*

The Fountain

A man stands by a moonlight water
Beneath a flickering star
And hears the water murmur
In the dark, as if necessity,
A maiden by invention caught,
Were taught against her will
To mother the smooth vowels
At night, where water mulls
Its matter to the frogs,
To the malignant toads
Caught in the rippling shadow.

Follow me, follow me, reader, and closely,
Not logically, that would be boasting,
But closely, closely; a breath of intention
Of beauty; a hoard guarded in famine.
An eluctable sound, or a word too loose
Would be a Haman, obtuse,
Persistent, tying his noose
Under an Esther's window
To hang like a treasoned lark
By the throat, under a lewd,
Under a lewd and gibbering window.

He stands beside an English water,
Hears a word like an Italian sound
Say "beauty" or a Spanish vowel; a gibberish
Of melodic lines, too smooth to jar
The night or make heard music
More than a tale of water chirping,
Wise as a bird, perhaps, or lewd,
Lewd as a widow, rude as a frog,
Or harsh as an alien voice
Speaking improbable verse,
And gaunt, in the fountain's shadow.

*

The Fulcrum

The letter "I"
Begins
With self-pity.

The very first cry
Of the human dunce
Notes the disparity

Between the estimation
He arrives with
And the perturbation

He survives with.

Perhaps the discovery
That the first person
Is not singular

Leads to recovery.
But that first aspersion

On his particular
Merits
Swells the pity

He inherits.

Pity for the letter "I"
That gleaming pillar

Of the entire plan,
The jewelled fulcrum
Of the wobbling man.

*

Gadarenes

This year, my pigs grew quickly,
Fed grossly, grew fat and grand as oxen,
Would have brought considerable money
At market.

The day before yesterday,
They were snuffling the roots
Of the enormous oak
At the edge of the cliff,
Happy as swine,
Filthy, muddy, hot with sunlight
And with lust.

All of a sudden,
Because one strange man
Wanted to be holy,
Intended to be holy,

Hup! Hup!

Insane.

*

The Garden

I

They came to an agreement with their morning,
Rose out of bed and out of darkness
With dawn like a dream in the sky
Of many colors to be proud before;
Rose to the longest morning of their lives.

II

The dog-star pointed Venus as an omen...
It would be long, this longest of mornings,
Repeating through hours without clocks
The forms and motions of the closing days
Decked in the colors of sleep and of morning.

III

The park began as does a Sunday, dawning
With leaves on the trees, turning to sunlight;
The mild-mannered children, abroad
In Sunday atmosphere as mild as plums,
Walked in the fruitful garden, easy-hearted.

IV

And park began as in a coppice, dreaming,
They saw light dancing, figuring darkness,
Or vanishing symbols of red,
Or possible couches, burdens of pleasure,
The blossoming plum and luxuriant branches.

V

The light of the dog-star came on them
Shone on a dream arching toward evening,
On a coiling and animate snare
That glowed round their bed like an adder
And whispered, and whispered impossible adage:

VI

"The scenery is changeless and perfect;
Trees, parakeets and plums are the future
Nor fade with inconstancy out
To spires, crosses, dragons with red teeth
Rolling their eyes— and morning held in abeyance."

VII

The snare, like the serpent in the picture
Bent, and flickering Venus
Watching the circular trap
That holds in its teeth the last morning
Shone, and with prescience, alive as an adder.

VIII

The dog-star pointed the place like a symbol,
The arc and inflexible steel over danger,
Over the bed and the dream
Where the amiable, nerveless grandparents
Mildly chatted of fruit and of bargains.

IX

And walked, as if chastisement were a promise
Given to children, easily altered,
And easily turned to delight.
Talked in the garden, brave as their splendor,
Witless and god-like in the bright dawn.

X

Talked! Perhaps of night and their dreaming,
Of promising light and fortuitous symbols,
Talked, until critically bent,
Venus in a chastening starlight
Tripped down the longest morning of their lives.

*

Grammar

Gently move the covers. Let the storm
Speak to our dear silence. Cuddle down.

Stillness is a kind of part of speech.
Watching the sun go down today in Persia—
The strangeness for us of so strange a place
Where clouds, preparing storm, were red and blue,
Turned our silence to a pause in song.

Pigeons and dust— detail upon detail—
The toppled chimney in the wind— are words.

Our bed time in a Persian, silken bed
Away from the hot anger of the sun.
The rising storm, the branches, pummeled leaves
Scraping our window, flying weakly past,
And our unhurried love are parts of speech.

We cuddled down at the ingathered rage,
Arms about and kisses; then a sleep
Long past innocence, askew and sound;
Silence in the bedroom, storm without—
Altogether speechless, done, amazed.

What about language? Will you really ask
If there was muttering in the fretful dark?

In the morning, when you lift your head,
There will be neither birds nor rain—
Only the empty morning after storm,
And goats and camels and a shivering hen
Pluming her ragged feathers in a daze.

*

Hart Crane— A Note

Perhaps Hart Crane
Took it unkindly that the sea
Hid him so completely;

And that, on his behalf
It did not split itself
To keep him dry for us

As once it split for those
Pernicious Israelites
Who haggled with their god so tediously.

Hart shook no recognition out of Him.
Instead, wet bones of poet sinking into sea,
The cold moved on to squid— and to anemone,

Without more inconvenience to the Lord
Than tide and bones moving from drift to sand
To slattern death in the unwounded sea.

*

Heinrich von Kleist and Henrietta Vogel

Henrietta Vogel took a walk.
The cavalier beside her had a gun—
It was a pistol, if we are precise.

They took a stroll; they rowed around the lake;
Had coffee, had a nap, a nip of rum.
And then he shot her. He was Heinrich Kleist.

She died, her breast exposed. Her family,
Like his, deplored the scandal that he made
When his bullet traveled through her heart.

She fell and slept beside a hollow tree
Beside the Wannsee in a little glade.
Then a servant heard a second shot.

Heinrich and Henrietta chose to fall.
She had a cancer; he had something else:
First, a genius Goethe labeled "rough",

Next, an officer's good aim, and best of all
That irritable kind of brain that spills
In hollow trees when it has had enough.

*

Helpless, Samuel Johnson
Composes A Letter to A Young Suicide

Your desires were too hot to brook delay;
You liked self-murder better than suspense.
Ah me— you make a wicked kind of sense,
Poor girl, to die enamored of the heat,
Nor risk a passion cooling day by day
Until you are a haunch of tepid meat
And lukewarm kisses swimming in pretence.

Perhaps the poignard is the best device
To slide between young ribs to keep them warm.
Ardent girl! You took your own advice
And died before you cooled into more harm
Than death could master, and your fiery knife
Kept you burning, while you burned, with life.

*

It is Time to Denounce

It is time to denounce the hallucinations
Of language.

For twenty years I have been after an image
And breath.

I have thought of the adder's tongue, and the peacock's
Daily.

The nightingale, also, occurred to me nightly,
Nightly.

It was a useless endeavour, I strained my voice,
I croaked.

There was a young woman, who when she spoke,
Pearls fell.

Her envious sister, stealing the secret
Spoke toads.

It is time to denounce the hallucinations
Of language.

*

Jasper

No city owns him more than each that holds
Him for a while. In each, his clothing moulds
A little more; his cautious manner thins
And he gives way to the compelling whims
Of the engrafted worm whose orders he
Obeys each year with more fidelity.
In jail, his jailers feed him; men of god
Explore his conscience while the doctors prod.

A man. His eccentricities belie
The way he grew. The clear, unscheming eye
For the dense country where the fir trees grow,
The land of thousand lakes, the tossed canoe
Below the flashing rapids, swimmers, girls,
High-heart Americana where it whirls
The pristine water; but the speckled trout
With their dull noses found his secret out.

He is the shy well-wisher to the world,
The quintessential uncle; gnarled
His workman's fingers; his pellucid eyes
Hide nothing, but reveal it, too; he plies
The gazing children of a neighborhood
With more than candy, but with less than food,
Until they know him as a man whose age
Explains his odor, but whose hands outrage.

He lives forever; when he comes to die,
That odor changes into sanctity.
His worm uncoils, but in Wisconsin fall
The waters proper to his funeral.
In those he kissed and swam. In those, the trout
With their blunt noses found his secret out;
There, before that coiling, noseless Death
Who relishes corruption, held his breath.

*

The Jewel

The jewel in the forehead of the toad,
No matter what the dry amphibian
Of the expense of beauty claims,
Unparalleled of gems will not erode.

Crouched he is, and amorous, and swart,
And to the sticking point batrachian,
His touchstone to the friendliest white hand
Egyptian darkness means, or squalid wart.

The carbuncle the creature wears
Will not erode. It is the steady mark
Of Abel's brother, the enlarged expense
Of the hot infamy they share

Against destruction. Soft, the jewel glows,
And guards a splintered lightning in the dark
Where it may work until its pieces,
Stronger than a cripple, strike again.

*

The Jongleur

Equipped with a portion of the dictionary,
A voice tending toward tenor,
And a fixed quantum of the world's dismay:
The jongleur!

A brevity of madness, as if one blind man
Led by the hand a boy
As perfectly as blind as he
And cried, "The sun!"

Still, a chorus of strings struck by fists
Armed with absolute desire,
Armed, also, in the dark, with absolute
Grief

Might (in the presence of flutes and wind
Passing over lips
That tasted honey)
Do it.

*

July

She puts the basket down
In the hot sun.

Cherries, grapes, a pear
And plums are there.

She bends above the fruit
Sleepy and mute

And feels the glowing sun
Assert its own,

In all things make a stir,
But most in her.

*

Just Deserts

More than perfection, more than the best
That is bearable is what we here deserve.

Listeners to music know this. Readers
Of the poem that resounds against

The hurt tympanum till it dreams
A moment stolen from the bitter truth

Know this. Anyone who climbs the mountain
Ranges, cowering away

From lassitudes of love, knows this;
And diggers of obtrusive graves.

Yesterday, because the rain fell on
And on, because the rain, coming from heaven

Swelled and poured for hours and hours on end
And I could, in the bedroom where I lay

Expect that I would sleep alone, and could
Achieve that expectation while the drumming

Rain reminded me of my success
At so much solitude, I said it too,

Between the raindrops and the thunder— said
It, wrote it, dreamed it all night long.

✳

Land's End

I sat at land's end, fishing. Out at sea,
A storm was blowing up; a cloud as large
As an extinct horizon, gathering.

I sat at land's end, fishing. My line dropped
Into the ocean, and I peered for fish.
The storm was distant, yellow, gathering.

Gathering like dust— gathering.
The sun was a grain of barley behind smoke,
Worn to a flickering glimmer in the sky.

I heard a rustling as the ranks of waves
Came to attention in long paper rows,
Their paper noses pointed up, like seals.

The shore was white; there were no clocks; the moon
Stood like an empty fishbowl in the sky.
I saw a gull climb toward it, wallowing.

I sat at land's end, fishing. My eyes burned
Backward in the smoke. My thin silk line
Dropped like a surgeon's thread into the sea.

Then there was Behemoth, an inch off shore,
Humped like the Urals, saying, "Reel
Your line in fisherman, for you've caught me."

"I won't", I said. "My line's too thin for you.
Swim off. You'll bruise the sun. Another inch
And all my coast is ruin. Swim away."

His crown shook like a forest made of bones;
The sun behind it flickered like a grain
Of barley as he answered, "You've caught me."

"Behemoth is bigger than the world", I said.
"He's blacker than a world without a sun.
His eyes are emeralds. He cannot see."

There was a turning of his craggy flukes
And the Antilles drowned. His emerald eyes
Converged upon the sky. He said, "See me."

I stood. I looked. I cried, "You're only meat.
I have a knife for meat. I have a knife..."
I heard the clatter of a barley seed

Skittering down the sky. "Is it now dark?"
Asked Behemoth. "It's very dark", I said.
"Your eyes have stared the sun into the sea."

I could not watch the sea-gull in the sky
Until the paper waves burst into flame—
I saw its wings above the blazing sea.

I saw a cicatrice against the sky
From which the seagull fell. I saw the stars
Turn ashen as it dropped; I heard them hiss

Like water quenching birds that burn. I saw
The darkness glowing like an emerald eye.
"All that you see", said Behemoth, "is me."

As if a fish had screamed, I screamed. I closed
My pocket knife and waited for the scar
Forming in the sky to stop its flow.

It stopped. I said, "I am a fisherman
Sitting at land's end. There are no fish.
What shall I do?" I said. "What shall I do?"

Behemoth, an inch off shore replied,
"You are a fisherman. Reel in. Reel in."
I spun my clicking reel. I reeled him in.

✳

Learning to Imitate Sleep

Now that a bone-white hawk
No longer darts from the sky

To tear at my chest; to steal
My heart as a gift for you;

Now that the crow has stopped
Tasting my nerve of devotion;

And the great whale's thirst at sea
Is partially quenched with my soul;

Now that my bed is not on fire,
And my arms are finally empty,

I am learning to imitate sleep.
Soon, I will imitate dreaming.

*

A Letter from Bali

I

All I can get this tropic dark to do
Is pour a rush of love I did not earn.

It swirls around me as if it would wet
My heart and lips, but I grow parched beneath

The stars that shimmer like bright snowflakes on
A hill. I cringe, I crimson. I begin

To stammer through my dreams. They swell
With faces that I never kissed with love.

Like hers— the thin, mad girl who said my name.
Clawing my cheek, she asked, "Why should I die

Before you'll let me cuddle you to sleep.
Only my brain, my dear, is mad. My breasts

And lips are sane. Why won't you love my flesh
And make a saint of me? Hello? Hello?"

My head burned like a crown of fires for her.
I smiled, and she was torn away by men

Who made apologies as if her cry
Of love had in it anything insane.

II

If only the moon would shine. I might survive
A night like this. If only I might dig

My head into the ground. When first she came,
Entranced and happy to my arms to die

She offered sprays of lilac I refused.
Later, she offered dogwood, cherry pinks,

And when all these were spurned, she chose
To come with empty hands into my heart,

Where I allowed her grief the little room
She needed for a while to kiss and cry.

She was the loser, and it's what she said,
But never added up the score I keep:

A girl gone mad; a scratch against my cheek,
And flesh I never wantoned with through nights

In which my poems were sustained by loss
As dark as Lethe and like Lethe, dumb

With all the ocean waiting until you
Nodded your head and floated off. Goodbye.

*

Mask for A Prologue

"There are possibilities for me, certainly,
but under what stone do they lie?"
—*Franz Kafka*

I

The stream of Iowa, the nightfrost clamped
Across the fields where houseless dogs remark
Without conviction, wanderings. The moon
On Hamlet's uncle shines; that busy Dane

Is mask and effigy whose husk is cramped
Against the stable door. His nephew, stark
As the arched angle of his eyebrows, croons
Into Ophelia's grasses: columbines

And daisies; fennel; rue among the thistles
Wilts beneath his buskins. Like a fool,
Lear slanders heaven in a frost-bound field
And treads the dying gentians with his heels.

Those blue-flowers feed the boar whose bristles
Gleam between the corn; inside, the cruel
Queens take sloven lovers, pant and yield
Their mouths and secrets while the empire reels.

II

Under what stones they lie, the kings and queens,
The rankling princes of the possible.
The scrawny lamb and the intrusive boar,
The bold, impetuous kine along the bank

Mark tragedy. The god of the machine,
A helpful genius of the visible,
Protects no farmer from the night. The hoar-
Frost was his flaw; now pride and rank

Luxuriance of leaping queens. The tame
Declining river from its sources crawls
Across the plains. The local bedroom keeps
The scent of stone and straw, the must of old

Intelligence, imposture, and the shame
Of retribution from on high. The farmer falls—
A great good man in Iowa whose sheep
Are nuzzling blue-flowers in a chilly fold.

III

That genius of the possible, Macbeth,
No shepherd was; but Agammemnon in a robe
Of wool lay down and died. The farmer's wife
Spins on the prairie neither gold nor wool;

She knows what tales are threadbare; saves her breath
Till her Aegisthus speaks, then smiles and stabs
Her lord and master, and her carving knife
Confirms a legend when his bath is full.

The tragic muse behind its mask appears
Dainty and dangerous; a pigpen squeaks
Varieties of shoat; the river glides
A mute antistrophe among the trees

Where two ghosts walk whose dying made them peers:
The king and farmer. In the darkness creaks
A palace or a bathroom door. Each hides
A great good man brought lower than his knees.

IV

In Iowa, the blue-flowers shrink. The crow
Down from the tower darts; the falling house
Beside the river, and the loosened hounds
Lean in the autumn wind. The possible

In the slack river lurks. The farmer's plow,
Now he is tragic where his cattle browse,
Lies helpless in the soil. Aegisthus pounds
The boards, and in the farmer's bed, the full

Sweet-scented sheet of their inclement lust
Makes gay their nostrils where the lovers lie.
Old Lear goes frantic, and the limping king
Inaugurates his blindness with his queen's

Unwinking brooch. Aloft, on Danish dust,
Over the hapless prince, the eagles fly,
Over the farmer, crows, whose posturing
His body libels as the play begins.

*

Miss Pettigrew

"I'm an artist— so don't bet on me."
—Maxwell Gordon

We learn, we learn that the lady in the picture
That we saw as children may be real.
Do you remember how she looked— the unbound
Chestnut hair tossed in the wind; her robes
Flowing, and a distant lark high
Upon the far horizon; flowers in
Her hand, the tallest meadow grasses waving
At her feet, and sky, indulgent to
The wistful clouds above her head?
How could we help but love her? She was lovely,
Lovely and she lived inside the gold
Imagination of the picture frame,
Gone rapt and beautiful— without a name.

But she is real; she's Margaret Pettigrew.
Yesterday, we saw her stand against
The sun upon that hill, her chestnut hair
Tossing in the wind, her summer gown
Rustling in the breeze and pale gray eyes
Fixed on the far horizon. In her hand,
Wild flowers, wild flowers in a cluster shone.
This time, the indulgent lark sang
A melody among the clouds in praise
Of Margaret whom we loved and called, but she
Turned her back on us and ran to meet
The gentleman she waited for whose name
Escaped us in a rush of blood and blame.

✳

Monsieur Chauvannes

Monsieur Chauvannes maintains a dark *ménage*
À trois, but in Des Moines; the persiflage
That from his chamber issues spoils the rest
Of stolid deacons in the middle west
Where two is company and three a crowd
Perhaps more glorious, but not allowed.

Back from Dubuque and to his ladies, home
The Frenchman hurries and his neighbors come
To watch his hallway and each other's eyes
For thin betrayals of the same surmise
That keeps them yearning until overhead
Sounds the weird skip-skipping of his double bed.

Those who grow corn and those who sorghum press
Are sometimes troubled by the same distress
Wherefore they writhe in bed or pace the floor
Who suffer with one wife and need one more;
They hear Chauvannes and his spry ladies tumbling;
The sounds of peril and of deacons stumbling.

*

Myself

What songs to sing, what flowers to offer!
The lilac, struck at midnight by the wet
Branch of the catalpa slashed by wind.

Canzones, canzones, canzones— or a song
That any mother might mistake
For love down in the valley where she sang.

Out of the brook the thirsty fish fly up
To flip their tails against the passing moon
Announcing to the midnight they are trout.

Down in the meadow there is moss upon
A slender stone, and there's a bug-eyed newt
That stares below the darkness. That's a song.

Oh kisses. Kisses. Drink up water, drink.
There is a tooth, there is a hand— a claw.
I bend over these lips, this voice. I sing.

I pound the meadow; I invent the crow.
I send the lovely mother toward the sun.
How headlong is my music; how intent

The linnet pasting feathers in her nest.
There slides the newt; here skip the trout and there
The lilacs drop their petals in the dark.

*

Omens

For a long while, we told ourselves
That the omens were good— the ocean was
Getting warmer. We got into the habit
Of thinking our civilization was moving into
A new serenity—calm waves, warm water—
Even an influx of sharks into our bay
Was welcome.

That winter, for the first time
There was no snow. Someone got us to plant
Seedling palms and we thought of plowing up
Our wheat to turn our valleys into citrus
Orchards.

When our children darkened
In the sun, we began to whisper that
The old gone garden was come round
Again, or soon would come. Someone recalled
An ancient prophecy that said the serpent
Would recoil upon himself before
That garden could spring up around us, and
Indeed, the common snakes died out
In that strange winter.

Slowly, we began
To think of innocence again. The warmth
Of spring was like a noonday dream; we dozed
Like unripe fruit beneath the sun. We put
Our furs away, our woolen suits, and learned
To sleep in linen, lightly, with our palms
Curled together.

When strident parrots came,
Early in the summer to the public
Squares, we did not mind their quarrels with
The frightened pigeons. Even the sudden flight
Into our northern city of flamingos
We received with joy. All things appeared
Benign. For a moment, also, the
Volcano that one morning thrust its cone
Innocently skyward in the bay.

*

On Carley Ridge

I went looking in the western foothills,
In the country of the deer and the coyote,
I, the Jew, tripped over manzanita
And disturbed the wooddoves, wooddoves,
Lizards, rattlesnakes and quarreling squirrels.

I climbed alone into those hills,
A Jew, into the oaks and pines, to see
How gentile nature was, by how much sweeter
She than all my Jewish loves,
My Jewish quarrels.

Naked on a western hill, I cried,
"A Jew is but a man," but was surprised
In looking down, to see that I had lied,
Or had forgotten I was circumcised.

*

On Permanence

In no instance may the world be made
Beyond its present making—
Not by singers on dark shores,
Not by suns illuminating barrows,

Nor by rain, washing the salt into
The beaches of the sea;
Not by branches of that lilac
Whipping in the wind,

Nor by the oak on the horizon
Spreading its stern branches
Like hands against disaster
Saying "No". Not by the vessel

Bobbing downward to the center
Of the storm. Change says
To the waiting world, "You are
The edifice I am, and break."

*

On the Fragility of Heat

Perfidious tenderness of ecstasy
In summer when no blackbird made a stir
Beneath the sun to watch us kiss

A moment in July. Lost, longing, we
Clung sweetly in our cottons, where the burr
Of dragonflies along the river missed,

Busy as they were, the sound to wake
Us. Ah, we were entranced and dazed
And would not move out of our lovers' pose

Despite July and gnats enough to make
Our kisses tingle. Loverlike, amazed,
We bore the heat and insects as the rose

Supports the bee. Perfidious the pose!
All through July, whose afternoons
Quivered by a shore that sweetness glazed

We met and kissed. Till August, when a blackbird woke
My lady to the heat, and she was gone
Who, all one honied month, I doted on.

*

The Page

There's only yellow lamplight on my page,
And creature comfort in the rug and room.
My bed is warm, yet slowly, slowly rage
Yawns behind me, makes itself at home.

All I merely meant to do was read,
Not breathe a tiger's languorous, thick stench.
He leans against my head his massive head,
Against my backbone his enormous haunch.

He purrs, and turns the razors in his pads
To sleepy digging, like a drowsy cat
Till what I read becomes a string of beads
As cruelly tangled as a Gordian knot.

*

The Partners

—For Delmore Schwartz

I

Fainthearted with being a Californian in
The city of New York, I listened to
The famous poet telling me his troubles
On Washington Square. His troubles. His
Shoes were being shined; the August sun
Early in the morning had a taste
Of dew; and under foot the pavement felt
Sticky with dismay. Poets are
Bad partners of delight and shame. Why should
This fearful rider on a stronger horse
Who clattered up the hill of glass cry down
To me for consolation; let him cry?

II

I did not let him cry. There is a trick
The soul performs within the flesh that makes
Us try for sainthood. The sun
Had been compassionate to me, and I
Had not deserved it either, so I bent
My head and listened while his shoes were shined
And his hurt diction, like a rain

Of heated stones came tumbling round my head
Harming us both with mock humility
And me with envy; I could not spare,
Despite my posture of humanity,
Even the smallest offering of love.

III

I bent my head and listened. In the Square,
Babies were being wheeled; a Negro tore
A biscuit into bits for pigeons, I watched
A girl more comely than a temperate dawn
Smile for a moment as she passed, while I
Ached with sainthood and the suave desire
To hold her in my arms. Meanwhile, his voice
Picked its way among the lava beds
Of his old griefs. I had my own, my own—
But it was I who paid to see his shoes
Shine on the pavement where he walked, while mine
Scuffed like prison boots the city stone.

*

The Peasant

Six times faster than the fool can weep
His passions trick him. When he's dry,
The urban peasant kills his tender sheep
That, softly, on his pillow pass him by.

This much Manhattan does. The bulky swain
In Harris tweed takes more than can be borne
Until he howls at night because his brain
In undervalued and his nerves are worn.

He counts his goods or counts the throats of sheep
Or murmurs to his soul, "My soul, be still."
But there's no gully deep enough to keep
The helpful yearlings that his passions kill.

An average man, the pavement where he walks
Is tough and bearable, but every night
The city slicker on his pillow balks
Before the switch that must turn out the light.

Barefoot and trembling, he will not be held
Accountable for murder in his sleep;
"It is not I—" his country cousin yelled
"Who cuts the gentle jugulars of sheep."

*

Poetry Reading

I crossed a bridge,
Drove thirty miles
To be greeted
By their smiles.

I read my poems,
Gave all I had
To please them and
To make them sad.

I let them see
The world I see:
Part pain, part love,
Part ecstasy.

I was vibrant,
I was great
With poems I knew
Were up-to-date.

And they were young,
Caught by my power.
I held them close
For one sweet hour.

But when I stopped,
Although the mood
I finished in
Had seemed so good

Nobody said,
"Stay for a drink,"
Or told me I
Had made them think.

Of all the pretty girls,
Not one
Said, "But the night
Is just begun."

Soft and lovely,
What they said
Was, "Gosh, we thought
That you were dead.

How nice you're not.
We're glad you came.
For years we've mis-
Pronounced your name."

I drove away,
I crossed the bridge
And wondered if
Noblesse oblige

Required my poems
Or me to die
To earn their fragrant
Young, "Goodbye."

*

Portrait of a Gentleman

These are the fingertips that may not pray,
And here the forgeries I shape at night;
This the mirror where the light of day
Chills impeccably to frosted light.

Here's my forehead in which all the world
Trots or gallops as I nod or beck:
These the temples in which reason's curled
Enough to play the world a master trick.

Here, my eyes, impetuous and blue
As diamonds poised against a pane of glass;
My lips are red as those that Adam knew,
Suave and gleaming from their first trespass.

Down below, I have a private part,
And the accoutrements enlivening it;
They serve me often as a kind of heart
Since mine is vacuum surrounding wit.

From top to toe, my mirror shows a man
Well-made, well-balanced, well-instructed, who
Armed with madness and a master plan
Does exactly what he needs to do.

*

Prologue to a Circus

The circus roars behind the brain
The skull's tight company from birth,
Has its recess and habitude
Between the spirit and the blood.

It trains the lion and the curly snout
To tricks the jungle may deny;
In darkness, dims the feral life
Or else comes on it in full cry.

The circus in the tight, round skull
Rattles havoc from the small redoubt;
From tarmac to the grave it knows
What all the shouting is about.

The circus in the formal haze
Shines reflections of the claw
That, gilded by its gold, divides
The perfect from the jungle law.

The Bengal tiger in the light
Bereaves his sense, leaps through the flame;
The tiger singes every day
To keep the headstrong jungle tame.

Locked, locked, the swagger in the blood;
The gaunt hyena in the dark
Breaks leaping from its narrow place
To be a tiger in the public park.

*

Rattler: On Carley Ridge

This morning, snake, the diamond rattler, on
The stone before the pool at which I drink.
I guess I should have left him there. I guess
That he is beautiful, and yet, my hair

And heartbeat warned me, and I reached my gun
Against his throat and fired. He did not sink
Simply to death, but slid into the grass
To thrash about. I tried to shoot him there

But held an empty rifle in my hand
And no more shells. I panicked. Hating snake,
The diamond skin, the rattles and his size,
The waving, wounded neck, the poisoned head,

I leaped to murder him. I stooped and found
The nearest weapons that should break
His skull and flung my rocks at his bright eyes,
And cursed and flung them, but he was not dead

For a long time, while I struck on and on,
And still he writhed, waving his head at me
As if to point the way out for the stone
With which, at last, I killed him. Now, I see

Him silent, limp and cold. Intricately bent,
And partly broken, he is beautiful
If dead; and I have kept the faith; I sent
My rocks, my gun, my heel against his skull.

*

A Rite of Spring

I saw her pause, though she was not a doe
Bending by a pool to drink. She was
The higher prey, the woman I adored,
For whom with sighs and prayers I set my snare
Where in a moment it would dazzle her.

Still later, sitting on a wet, dark stone,
I heard the forest calling me a fool
Who pursed his lips and kissed the empty air.
I felt a swarming music in my loins—
As if an anthill might be whistling me.

Each way I turned the forest played back notes
I could not stand to hear because bereft;
A woodpecker attacked three voiceless grubs;
A blue jay yammered at a yammering squirrel;
A wild canary whirred across the pool

Where she was lost. Ah Love, I set my trap
With all the skill a lover can command;
And yet she's free, she's fled out of the woods
In which undazzled she eluded me
And left me dangling, dangling in your snare.

*

Shiraz: The Desert

Stars keep their distance from the Persian night.
The hills depend for definition on
The moon and movement. Sometimes a lynx
Stirs the denser shadows, but the true

Fauna are the feeble mice that shake
The dry grass underfoot. They hunt and catch
What little nothing crumbled in the sun
And dust. Persia is a country hot

By day and mystified and cool at night:
Always a nervous rustling among leaves,
Always a sense of distance from the stars
And danger, mildly waiting near a cave.

It is a dumb horizon, where all shapes
Turn oriental in the dark: a lynx,
A shepherd driving sixteen sheep. When dawn
Breaks upon the line of hills, the stars

Will be aloof against that light, as now,
Keeping their distance, they ignore the mice
That feebly feed their generations here,
Treading with fitful weight, the seed husks down.

*

Siren

Police or fire? We've been in bed because
Of weariness and love; but it's not safe.
Our sheets have lost their warmth, our pillows twist—
Someone's injured; someone's breaking laws.

Drowsy perfumed and beautiful, you lie
No longer fast asleep; the night has lost
All that the dark keeps commonplace and clean,
All the stillness that we slumber by.

Ambulance or fire— what's the news?
The stars are cut by gimlets and their light
Shines on kittens in cold alleys where
Someone stumbles, someone else pursues.

Sleep's the privilege we may not own
However we deserve it. Take my hand
And hurry, darling, while we have a chance
To steal a roadmap; to get out of town.

*

The Sleeping Beauty

What was the heartache he intended healing?
On a Monday morning, see him mount
And turn his charger to the eastward hills
Where lies his princess, waiting for her wedding
Behind brambles thick with nightingales.

Once past brambles, thick with nightingales,
He climbs the stairway to her musty chamber
Where she lies sleeping on an iron bed.
He breaks her windows so that madrigals
May drift across her lovely, drowsy head.

He bends to kiss her lovely, drowsy head,
And dozes, caught up in a tedium
Made half of perfume, half of burning briar,
A sleepy incense rising from her bed
Warmed in the thicket of her own desire.

Lost in the thicket of his own desire,
He does not notice when his princess dies,
But feels an absence that requires concealing.
He takes her, mounting to the topmost spire,
A brambled staircase as the light is failing.

He mounts the staircase as the light is failing,
And puts his princess on a rusty bed.
He lies beside her, while the nightingales
Rise, like vessels to misfortune sailing
That darken all the ocean with their bells.

*

Songs for a Grandfather

I

The hen clucks for hers, and when
The human offspring makes its torn
Departure from the night there is

An outcry. Why are children born
When we are half asleep and press
Blind pillows for our dreams?

What kinds of little fires caress
Our God in heaven. Does He warm
His fingers? Does He wait for sleep?

II

The child is born. The world is hushed
And still. In such a winter, who
Can hear the German knife go snick?

The circumciser leaves the new
Citizen of pain behind
Him mad and howling in the dark.

He takes some flesh along— a kind
Of souvenir of meat and grief
Cut from homunculus, lost

And lovely in a handkerchief,
Gone red and white, like roses.
Who knows what he will do with it?

He may wait till the low moon passes
And hold it up, like a mistake
To ask the blessing of a tear.

Or else, he'll bury, like a sick
Comedian, his joke inside
A hole where it will giggle on.

III

Homunculus' family
Sits around the stove. It sings
Ragged music, like a song.

Father makes a sound like things
That break: Dishes, hinges, kitchen
Sinks— watertaps and mirrors.

Mother studies groaning in
Her corner. The country of mistakes
Is where she lives, by joy embittered.

Brother sits, inventing headaches
To improve the hours between
His stanzas of the family song,

While sister, passionate and virgin
Gathers rusty iron daisies
On the tundra of her dreams.

Grandma, behind greedy eyes
Counts children she has had and spoiled,
While grandpa, on his back, counts stars.

IV

Stunned into breathing, the moist child
Drinks milk. Around his pliant bones,
Nights curl and cling. He sucks and grows,

Kicks at the shadows and complains
Because he cannot see the sky
Or understand the family song.

Sometimes he utters a small cry
Because his penis hurts. That note
Makes muted, if familiar, woe.

V

He counts the years, as children count,
Mingling hours with leaves and snowflakes—
The sunlight with the whirling wind.

Daily, the child is pleased and makes
The push the days require before
They fall into their cobwebbed well.

VI

Snowflakes do not know the law
Of number, but the child is young
And counts beside them as they fall.

They will not touch him, though his tongue
Burns for their sweetness, and his eyes
Glisten when the snowflakes melt

Or dazzle near him. When he tries
To catch them in his outstretched hands
He catches nothing for his pains.

One year, the snow befriends
The boy. It says, "Wait, until
I call for you." He bows and waits.

VII

The boy wakes up at night and hears
The boarder pounding on his bed
Inside his brightly lighted room.

The raging blind man cries out, "God,
I'll teach you to be blind. I'll show
You how it's done. Like this...and this.

I'll pound your brains out till you know
How to be blind. Don't hide from me
You stinking God! Why aren't you blind?"

VIII

The boy grows, wondering. His flesh
Creeps out and in. Homunculus
Enlarges, cell by cell, gets fed

Potatoes, cheese, asparagus.
At night, he squirms against the years;
By day, he laughs or moans or leaps.

He thinks he is part twitch, part ears,
Part elbow-pain, part knee, part youth,
Part toe, part sleep, part song.

In moments of exquisite truth,
He tries to undo his belly button,
Making the acquaintance, at

An early age of Kant, Cro Magnon
Man, Pythagoras, Plotinus,
Shakespeare and the Pope of Rome.

IX

One morning in July, the boy
Looks out on a heap of cinders.
Standing on a porch, he drinks

Cool water, sees the sun scratch colors
In the slag— the vanished glows
Of its last burning, red and green.

There's a puff of wind. It blows
Across Lake Erie and it brings
The scent of apples mixed with tar.

X

Late at night, as if it were
The hour to be born, a tree
Trips upon its roots and falls

Against the house and family.
Vast and evergreen, it splits
The upper rooms and attic, tears

Its way through alcoves where the rats
Maintain their rights and privacies.
The tree breaks windows, punches walls

And wakes the father up who cries,
"My God! A new expense." The tree
Groans and is its own excuse.

Ready with her misery,
Mama rings her little bells
Of pain. "Oh," she says, "Oh my."

The brother spits out particles
Of tree and laughs. This late at night
He had no plans for bitterness.

Sister keeps her eyes closed tight
And grinds her teeth while she explores
The lava beaches of the dream

Of midnight madness that was hers
To tickle for a while. Now rigid,
She feels the six-foot branch of tree

Lying beside her in the bed.
It must weigh forty pounds and hurts
Her pride because the damn thing's smiling.

What is bald grandma doing— what
Should grandma ever do? She tells
The broken walls that grandpa is

A fool. He wakes up, like a squirrel
And prays a little, like a sheep
That feeds on prayer and is content

With God. The boy, out of his sleep
Says, "Night, night" to the broken tree.
The wind moves in his hair, "Goodnight. Goodnight."

XI

In October, in the middle
Of the day, he thinks about
The moon and wonders if she is

His mother. Meaning to find out,
He stays awake all night to watch.
Indeed, she hurries by— like mother.

XII

The boy opens a door and looks
Inside a cottage crumbling on
A mountain next to water. There,

A crippled, gentile boy, far gone
Toward death, lies half-way dozing
On his dirty bed beneath

A cloud of flies. Outside, the splashing
Of a waterfall on stones.
Three soldiers come with forks to spear

The trout out of the brook that runs
Below the ruined house; the fish
Spurn at its narrow banks as forks,

Darting in the ripples, flash
Their tines like twisted silver, click
Against the rocks. The dying child

Keeps to his steady drowsing, sick
Beyond complaint or care. The sudden
Light that spills in at the door

Disturbs a singing cricket hidden
In a corner of the room. The flies
Are not disturbed; they know their song

And sing it while the gentile dies
As fish in the cold mill-race leap
Desperate, from the water— speared.

XIII

He grows. From time to time, glancing
At his little penis, he
Thinks there's something missing, or

Undone. As far as he can see,
The thing behaves according to
The rules he knows. At night, he thinks

He sees the shadow of a Jew
Who made a Jew with a sharp German
Knife. He thinks that he recalls

A sick comedian, a moon
Staring at a foreskin, pain
Like laughter on an empty shore.

XIV

One morning, the boy cries out,
"I won't grow any more. Down
With growing. I make a solemn vow

To be a child forever." When
He finishes, he thinks, "How fine
My voice is; that was lovely, splendid."

Too late, he learns how the occasion
Tells against him. Sitting down,
He finds his noble pants are wet.

XV

The boy decides one year that grandpa
Is a saint. Creeping up,
He looks into the old man's eyes

And sees a cancer, like a tulip
Growing shapely, venomous
And black inside the helpless pupils.

He whispers to his grandpa, "Pious
Jew, what will you say to God
When He's done grazing on your flesh?"

The old man smiles, "You've got a head
For questions; mine is busy with
The thing I know— the way to pray.

As for God's grazing, may my death
Give him good appetite." The boy
Cries out, "I will not let you die."

XVI

Ankle deep in the warm water
Of a sea, he hears the news
Come floating like a song written

In tangled wire: "This ocean is
Forever shallow. It will not deepen
Where you walk." Clearly, it's time

To find himself a better ocean
If he means to swim. He leaps
Naked and innocent into

Successive seas whose swelling deeps
Lap round his ankles while the wire
Tangles music in his ears.

XVII

His brother, turned comedian,
Puts a burr between his legs
And rides it, like a cowboy...on.

Worn out at last with love, he digs
A final hole and climbs into
It cheerfully and shuts his eyes.

XVIII

Once more, the boy tries snow. It falls
As always, all around him, slow,
Numerical, and white...aloof.

He wants the sky to turn to snow,
The moon to crystallize, the stars
To turn to snowflakes where they hiss.

He wants his God to leave disasters
And the drift of wars, to turn
Into a single snowflake, falling

Past great trees. To settle down
At last to His lost home— the tip
Of the aching boy's red tongue.

XIX

Mother runs amok. She eats
Green elderberry and she crows
As roosters crow who cannot tell

The time of day: "*Co co ri co*"
She cries, "I sing the bloody night
When infants pound the hidden door

And ask permission into light.
Myself", she cries, "*co co ri co*
I do not sing— nor all my sons."

The boy obeys this summons, too.
He carts her off— he locks her in
And gets a kiss, like elderberry.

XX

Falling out of bed at dawn,
He giggles at a dream of nests
And spiders in a cherry tree.

He dances all spring long with breasts
Both large and small, and watches birds
Build nests below which spiders hang.

He dances and his teeth chip words
That break like promises to girls,
Then rides the furious pony home

That lives between his thighs and curls
Around it in his pungent bed
And spits out kisses for his pillow.

XXI

Grandma dies of asthma and
A chicken bone stuck in her throat.
Wearing a brand new wig, she makes

A horrid corpse— as if a goat
Wrapped inside a judge's robes
Trundled to a marble grave.

The old-maid sister knits and sobs.
Her knitting needle at the funeral
Goes tic and ticatic and tic.

XXII

It's an old, old story and it goes
On and on and will not stop
Till grandpa slips away content

To hear at last God smack his lips
Pleased with so much dying
And the hum of honey bees.

The story's old. The boy's a man,
Somewhere always there's a song
That still needs singing at the end of day.

And so he sings it, though he's sometimes wrong
And sometimes right, as when he finds the snow
Poised melodious upon his tongue.

*

Sonnet: Halloween

Catalpas, maples, ginkos, elms and oaks
Grew in my childhood. Buckeyes spread their shade
On avenues I sometimes walked along
And there were forests in the tales I read.

Why then am I uneasy in these woods?
The fallen leaf, the taste of sadness from
The autumn bark, the humous under foot
And snapping branches in the undergrowth

Were never strange. These colors and the dim
Movements of the lowering afternoon
I've known for years. I am a grown-up. Soon,
Out of the scented ground will spring the old

Woman I remember best— the crone
I longed for always when the light was gone.

*

The Stone Cicada

I

Poetry is the language of a state of crisis,
The language of the stone cicada as it leans
Like the receiver of a spoken curse
Toward the speaker. The cicada
Is an artifact of jade, leaning toward sound;
A statue, leaning toward the hardly obtainable,
Until, at last, and perfectly— no! all
But perfectly, the fragile, oriental
Stone, fulfilling the intelligence
Of jade carved into wings may form,
Out of calamities of silence, sound.

II

Somewhere, an Asiatic nightingale is fixed
Into an attitude of music. Hooked
Against a thorn, it, tongueless, cries
A melody into the air.
So cried Lavinia in her throat, and held
Her miserable sanity between
Her teeth and swore upon the guilty stage
Revenge. Varieties of song!
So sing the redbreasts, twittering
About the dying worm; and on his way
To hell the hopeless Juan loved and sang.

III

Would sing! The oriental dynasty is dead
Which set the jealous eyes into that face.
The jade cicada's crisis waits.
The thin, dry mouth, where oriental
Languor stiffens to emotion, stirs,
Or seems to stir. Behind that polished mouth
Is said to be a tongue of ruby, carved,
Coiled, restrained, perfectly unseen,
A silent fillip in a tight display
Of the cool orient about to fly,
Almost— almost to fly— about to sing.

IV

The orient grown hot, equipped with wings
And lice, the orient that flew and coughed
Into no handkerchief sat on the steppes
And greased its hair with rancid butter, sang
Of love and clasped strange girls
In weird embraces, cried aloud and took
The filthy singer for the hidden song
Kept no silent stone. (Tamarlane
Stopped the bleating of a thousand lambs
A month to keep his kettle drums in tune
And took the world by storm— indifferently.)

V

The artifact would fly, the shapely stone,
The green cicada of Peking would roar...
If only the desire could subdue
The granite larynx where the weeping sound
Of desolation lives, or where it hides
Unroared, implicit in the ruby throat.
Poetry is the language of a state of crisis,
Of music and the mongol hordes returning
Sick with the melody Lavinia sang
When she was ravished, and Don Juan sick,
And the cicada with its pale green wings.

*

Stood the Arabian Arab Up to Sing

Stood the Arabian Arab up to sing...
Gave her voice all its dimensions,
Turned it loose over the world
To circle with the white doves overhead,
Circling on the green and marbled valley,
Turning like imagination's step
In the hot land in a part of Africa.

How the Arabian Arab sang;
The reeds split in her voice,
Dispersed like water her dimensions
Through the dry and rustling reeds,
Until each measure played a blind
And yearning music in the dark of Africa.

How long the dark Arabian sang...
Night took her by the voice and baffled her
In the white light of her dimensions,
Baffled her with music and with cold,
Till the disparate creatures of her voice
Rustled like white pebbles in dry reeds,
Rustled in her heart in Africa.

✳

Surgery for a Lady

The end of sickness then? Suppose my blood
Should fail to clot; suppose my heart is stilled,
My lymph is scattered, and I lie destroyed
Among the rubble of my nerve and bone.

I summon every sweetness I have known.
The caves of the Pacific, and the salt
Destruction of the channel waves: the hours
My son came hurt into the world from me.

My transitory lover, too— too swift
To be substantial. Like a goad, too hard
To be unreal, and therefore, like a kiss
Compact of tenderness and injury.

Fixed in a lassitude between a trance
And love, we swayed like weary eagles
Who have fought each other to a bitter cry
Of recognition on a ledge of sleep.

Our sweetness flowed along at least two rivers.
If, tomorrow, in such tides, my blood
Declines as then it flowed and ebbed, my flesh
Will grope the rim of darkness till it fails.

*

The Tailor: On Carley Ridge

Three deaths: the squirrel, the partridge and the dove.
Now he is a hunter on a ridge
Who lusted after flesh of his own killing.
And killed it. There's the trick that takes the city

Shine off, and here's the bloody hero of
Wild meat, the cosmopole for whom the partridge
Is a common bird, a chicken falling
At his will. Farewell the ghetto. Farewell pity.

If it bleeds, he's ready for
The whole creation: lizards, tigers, toads
And enemies. Esau was a hunter
And the line is not extinct, though Jacob

Cheated him. Three deaths! Henceforth, the food
Of one tough tailor will be spiced with blood.

*

To a Friend Who Decided to Die

You ached with troubles but their resonance
Taught you nothing on this dying star.
Sometimes you winked, as if within your eye
There burst out battles of a widening war

With men in trenches, women leaped upon
And sick battalions quartered in a school
Where you went round to kiss, to bind up wounds—
You, a warrior; you, a mark; a fool.

Which way you turned was no place, so you went
In all directions since they were the same.
What else was there to do if choosing was
Another chance to play a losing game?

Poor mark, poor fool, poor friend, do you suppose
Things will be better on some other star?
The ache is in our flesh right from the start:
The bullet that we bite is where we are.

*

The Tomb of Cyrus

This is the tomb of Cyrus. Here's a hole
Among the broken stones where camel drivers
Piss. The poppies spread out in the spring—
On every poppy there's a blast of sun.

Dry. Dry. The clay, the trees are dry.
Persia is a drouth upon the tongue.
A dust goes scudding toward Jerusalem.
Rising a moment from the empty tomb

It settles, when the fitful wind expires,
In skimpy mounds, in traceries, in cracks.
The poppies, under dust, decline their heads;
The lizards lick at it, alert and dumb.

O king. O king. How long the files of kings
Who brought their lambkins to Persepolis
To make your irritable lions roar—
Your justice blazed on them from lamps of stone.

The wind rises. In Persia there's a wind
For all occasions; now a wind to blow
Your mausoleum like a whistle. Thieves
Have emptied it; the Persian king is gone.

King Cyrus sent them to Jerusalem—
Those Jews, their cooking pots; their wives, their woes.
Parched, with the dust of Cyrus on their tongues,
They trudged toward secret fountains in the stone.

*

Were Horses Then Beggars

Well, suppose that I was really dead,
Lying in a Russian grave deep underground
With fingerfuls of moist earth stuffed
Generously in my ears and mouth.

Suppose me broken there and friendly with
The channering worm that eats the soil
Mouthful after mouthful of rich earth,
And me included in its meal as well.

Suppose me there in death, like one who fell
Beneath a fist of darkness; one whose brain
Froze, like a frightened clown, inside my skull
No longer leaping between pain and pain,

With lumps of humus slowly pressing on
My tongue, untasted; or a mash of oak
Or aspen scrapings, elm, a pinch of pine
Bark and twigs turned scrappy, wet and black.

Then suppose a gift— one miracle!
The only one allowed— what would I take
Except the steadfast power of keeping still
Or the relentless impulse not to wake.

*